Arthur Howard Galton

Two Essays upon Matthew Arnold with some of His Letters

to the Author

Arthur Howard Galton

Two Essays upon Matthew Arnold with some of His Letters to the Author

ISBN/EAN: 9783337241322

Printed in Europe, USA, Canada, Australia, Japan

Cover: Foto ©Thomas Meinert / pixelio.de

More available books at **www.hansebooks.com**

Two Essays upon
Matthew Arnold
with some of His Letters
to the Author

By
ARTHUR GALTON

LONDON: ELKIN MATHEWS
IN VIGO STREET
MDCCCXCVII

MRS. ARNOLD

NIL SINE TE MEI PROSUNT LABORES.

"Ουτοι ἀπόβλητ' ἐστὶ θεῶν
ἐρικυδέα δῶρα.

MATTHEW ARNOLD: HIS PRACTICE, TEACHING, AND EXAMPLE. A PROSE ESSAY ON CRITICISM

Nullum fere scribendi genus non tetigit;
Nullum, quod tetigit, non ornavit.

ATTHEW ARNOLD has gone away suddenly from us; and his departure is making us realize, with bitter sorrow, all that we have lost. If it were possible, in a single phrase, to define the work of a great author, that phrase, which I have chosen, out of Goldsmith's epitaph, might define the work of Matthew Arnold: "He laboured in almost every field of literature, and every-

I

thing, which he handled, became fascinating and beautiful." Definitions, however, cannot be more than weak efforts reaching towards the truth ; they are all bound to fall short, to press unduly upon a single aspect of it, to define it partially ; though, in this case, the first half of Johnson's epigram is, perhaps, entirely true: Matthew Arnold was a labourer "in almost every field of literature ; " it is this width of range, this universality of his, which gives him an unique position among contemporary men of letters : He "saw life steadily, and saw it whole."

But, though his touch has always the gifts of beauty, and has always fascination, he can endue things with even higher qualities than these. " Poetry," he says himself, " interprets by expressing with magical felicity the physiognomy and movement of the outer world, and it interprets by expressing, with inspired conviction, the ideas and laws of the inward world of man's moral and spiritual nature : " it interprets by having

2

"natural magic" and "moral profundity."
If Matthew Arnold's poetry be looked
at as a whole, it will not, I think, be
found wanting in " moral profundity ; "

> " Tears
> Are in his eyes, and in his ears
> The murmur of a thousand years."

His verse is penetrated with a grave and
a serious morality ; and, because he is
haunted by " the something that infects
the world," his verse, when he is de-
scribing the outward aspects of Nature,
is " drenched," as he would say, " with
natural magic : "

> " Not by those hoary Indian hills,
> Not by this gracious Midland sea
> Whose floor to-night sweet moonshine fills,
> Should our graves be.

> " So sang I ; but the midnight breeze,
> Down to the brimm'd, moon-charmed main,
> Comes softly through the olive trees
> And checks my strain."

But, in addition to the quality of "natural
magic," and to the expression of the
beauty and fascination of the outer world,

3

✓ there is in his verse an ever present sense of the largeness and of the austerity of Nature :

> "Thin, thin, the pleasant human noises grow,
>   And faint the city gleams ;
> Rare the lone pastoral huts—marvel not thou !
> The solemn peaks but to the stars are known,
> But to the stars and the cold lunar beams ;
> Alone the sun arises, and alone
>   Spring the great streams."

✓ It is this sense of austerity and of largeness, which gives him his finest inspiration ; and I should point to his expression of that sense, and to his application of it to "the ideas and laws of man's moral and spiritual nature," if I were asked to name his most individual and distinguishing quality. The following verse is an example of what I mean, and it will serve to mark the difference between Matthew Arnold and Wordsworth, in their treatment of Nature :

> "They
> Which touch thee are unmating things—
> Ocean and clouds and night and day ;
> Lorn autumns and triumphant springs."

4

Wordsworth's message to us from Nature is, that it is a sympathetic, a companionable thing; he says, for instance, in his *Tables Turned*:

> "Books! 'tis a dull and endless strife:
>   Come, hear the woodland linnet,
> How sweet his music! on my life,
> There's more of wisdom in it.
>
> ⚹ And hark! how blithe the throstle sings!
>   He, too, is no mean preacher:
> Come forth into the light of things,
>   Let Nature be your teacher.
>
> "She has a world of ready wealth,
>   Our minds and hearts to bless—
> Spontaneous wisdom breathed by health,
>   Truth breathed by cheerfulness.
>
> "One impulse from a vernal wood
>   May teach you more of man,
> Of moral evil and of good,
>   Than all the sages can."

And this impression of the joy that is to be found in Nature, of her living sympathy and companionship, is almost everywhere present in Wordsworth; it is the prevailing impression, that he leaves with us.

The prevailing impression, which we get from Matthew Arnold, on the other hand, is that Nature is a calming thing: calming from its austerity, from its obedience to unswerving laws, from its infinite patience, and from its " toil un-sever'd from tranquility."

" And a look of passionate desire
O'er the sea and to the stars I send:
Ye who from my childhood up have calm'd me,
Calm me, ah, compose me to the end!

" Ah, once more," I cried, "ye stars, ye waters,
On my heart your mighty charm renew!
Still, still let me, as I gaze upon you,
Feel my soul becoming vast like you!

" From the intense, clear, star-sown vault of heaven,
Over the lit sea's unquiet way,
In the rustling night-air came the answer:
' Wouldst thou *be* as these are? *live* as they.'

" Unaffrighted by the silence round them,
Undistracted by the sights they see,
These demand not that the things without them
Yield them love, amusement, sympathy.

" And with joy the stars perform their shining,
And the sea its long moon-silver'd roll;
For self-poised they live, nor pine with noting
All the fever of some differing soul.

6

"Bounded by themselves, and unregardful
In what state God's other works may be,
In their own tasks all their powers pouring,
These attain the mighty life you see."

In thus dealing with Nature, Matthew Arnold has a message, or an inspiration, of his own : up to a certain point, he follows Wordsworth ; and then he goes beyond him, and gives us something that Wordsworth has not given. I do not say something greater, than Wordsworth has given ; I only wish to point out, that it is something different. I do not compare the poets, I distinguish their qualities ; because one of the most essential, though the most neglected, functions of true criticism, is to seek out these finer shades of difference ; to extract the " peculiar sensation, the peculiar quality of pleasure which a man's work excites in us." And the very fineness of that sense, which can so discriminate, will make its possessor delight in these " peculiar qualities," and dwell in them ; but it will, at the same time, restrain him from

7

the common and the lamentable habit, of pointing to a distinction for the sole purpose of establishing a vulgar rivalry. For there is a school of criticism, which is employed continually in "placing the poets," or in "putting writers into the main literary current," whatever that may mean. Those critics, who employ this easy method of comparison have little to say about any individual poet, or about Poetry herself; their remarks, in consequence, are so vague and accommodating, that they may be applied with equal fitness to every poet, and to almost every writer. This, no doubt, is a wonderful triumph of ingenuity; but still, it has its disadvantages: the disadvantage for the critic is, that he is apt to lose sight of the fine distinctions between things, he is a little wanting in discernment; the disadvantage for the reader is, that he gains nothing definite, his notions are not cleared. The disadvantage for the poet, whom the critic wishes to explain, and the reader to study, is, that he is not revealed; he is certainly "put into the literary current," but he is overwhelmed in the flood of verbiage, which flows there. And when a writer talks of "placing the poets," there is only one thing to be done; that is, to place his own writing at once in the waste paper basket: The phrase is offensive, the thing is impossible, the desire for it is absurd. It is most of all absurd, offensive, and impossible in the case of a modern or of a living poet; for the history of literature tells us, very plainly, that no age has ever been able to estimate its poets with absolute truth and insight. Every age can, indeed, feel its own poets in a more penetrating way, than an alien time can feel them; but it cannot give so true a verdict about them. A poet may commend himself to his own age by some touch of sentiment or of style, which beguiles that age to over-estimate enormously his true poetical quality. He may, in like manner, be under-rated as a poet; not for any defect in poetry, but because he does not appeal in any special way to the prevailing sentiment of his time. And posterity, which will judge with a cool impartiality far removed from the passing contemporary sentiment, may entirely reverse, and quite justly reverse, the contemporary decision. It is only when an age has passed away, that its real function and its true place can be discerned; and, until that period arrive, the literature, which reflects any given age, cannot be judged finally. It is, therefore, premature to form any opinion about Matthew Arnold's relative position among his contemporaries. And we, who are touched ourselves by the same emotions and desires, which move the poets of our time, are as little able to realize the position they will finally take among the English classics; we cannot settle the order of their precedence in that great list; we cannot even tell, with infallible certainty, which of them will be found worthy to have a place in it at all.

" The epoch ends, the world is still.
The age has talk'd and work'd its fill—
The famous orators have shone,
The famous poets sung and gone,
The famous men of war have fought,
The famous speculators thought,
The famous players, sculptors, wrought,
The famous painters filled their wall,
The famous critics judged it all.
The combatants are parted now—
Uphung the spear, unbent the bow,
The puissant crown'd, the weak laid low.
And in the after silence sweet,
Now strifes are hush'd, our ears doth meet,
Ascending pure, the bell-like fame
Of this or that down-trodden name,
Delicate spirits push'd away
In the hot press of the noon-day,
And o'er the plain, where the dead age
Did its now silent warfare wage—
O'er that wide plain, now wrapt in gloom,
Where many a splendour finds its tomb,
Many spent fames, and fallen mights—
The one or two immortal lights
Rise slowly up into the sky,
To shine there everlastingly."

But, it may be urged, if the sphere of
criticism be thus limited, what do you
leave the critic to work upon, when he

may desire to form a judgment about contemporary poets; are a poet's contemporaries alone to have no definite opinion about his work? There was once a prudent French critic, who was incessantly haunted by " La peur d'etre dûpe; " he was in continual dread lest he should make a fool of himself, and this abiding terror controlled all his utterances. Now there is nothing in which a man can so easily make a fool of himself as in passing hasty and sweeping judgments upon his contemporaries. Of course we can all pass judgments upon them, and we like doing it immensely; though such judgments can only be useful to us, if they avoid all heated, partizan feeling; and if we clearly recognize how limited and tentative they must be, from the very nature of the case. But I think, decidedly, it would be better to form no judgments at all than to express, dogmatically and with no sense of hesitation, judgments which have every chance of proving false; like the judgments, effusive and exaggerated, or stinted and inadequate, which are poured out at the death of every man of letters, almost before he is cold, by the newspaper critics and reviewers. Never to think at all, would be better than to think like them ; for they think and write with no healthy dread before their eyes, with no controlling sense of fear, and they have to endure the penalty of being wholly unrestrained :

> "Misericordia e Giustizia gli sdegna;
> Non ragionam di lor, ma guarda e passa."

The serious critic, however, though he sternly limit his operations, and though he guard himself against every temptation to form a relative judgment, is left, after all, with sufficient matter upon which to exercise his intelligence. There are three things, which he can discuss with profit: he can discuss the poet's matter or substance; he can discuss his manner or style; and he can record that impression, which he makes upon a contemporary student. The latter judgment, when it is given honestly and with any real insight, will always be valuable and a most interesting legacy to future historians of literature; most interesting and valuable, perhaps, when the contemporary view differs widely from the final verdict; most gratifying to the shade of the critic, and the best to his penetration, when it differs but little from the ultimate verdict of posterity.

Before a critic is able to discuss with profit the substance or the style of a poet he must shun two faults which, in these days of ours, stultify a great deal of our criticism. He must avoid basing his judgment upon fragments or disconnected passages; he must be still more careful that he does not choose those fragments, because they are examples of what he may think, fine descriptions of natural scenery. "Descriptive poetry," says Mark Pattison, "is simply a contradiction in terms. A landscape can be represented to the eye by imitative colours laid on a flat surface, but it cannot be represented in words which, being necessarily successive, cannot render juxtaposition in space. To exhibit in space is the privilege in the arts of design. Poetry, whose instrument is language, involves succession in time, and can only present that which comes to pass under one or other of its two forms, action or passion." Or, as Mr. George Meredith has written, in better language and with finer thought: "The art of the pen (we write on darkness) is to rouse the inward vision, instead of labouring with a drop-scene brush, as if it were to the eye." Yet there are critics now, who will search through a poet for descriptions of scenery, which appeal to their individual sentiment; they will isolate these descriptions, and take them from their connexion; they will define them, perhaps, as "beautiful cameos of description;" and then, they will proceed to judge the poet's work by their estimate of these alone. Matthew Arnold himself shall expose this popular delusion, this widespread fallacy. Speaking of the "beautiful cameo" theory, of the insanity of judging a poem, or any work of art, by its scattered fragments, he says : " A modern critic would have assured him (Menander) that the merit of his piece depended on the brilliant things which arose under his pen as he went along. We have poems which seem to exist merely for the sake of single lines and passages, not for the sake of producing any total impression. We have critics who seem to direct their attention merely to detached expressions, to the language about the action, not the action itself. I verily think that the majority of them do not in their hearts believe that there is such a thing as a total impression to be derived from a poem at all, or to be demanded from a poet; they think the term a commonplace of metaphysical criticism. They will permit the poet to select any action he pleases, and to suffer that action to go as it will, provided he gratifies them with

16

occasional bursts of fine writing, and with a shower of isolated thoughts and images. That is, they permit him to leave their poetical sense ungratified, provided he gratifies their rhetorical sense and their curiosity." A poem, then, if we are to form a satisfactory judgment of it, must be regarded as a whole. It would be an example of un-intelligent criticism, for instance, to select a passage out of Matthew Arnold's *Tristram and Iseult*, a passage out of Lord Tennyson's *Merlin and Vivien*, and a passage out of Mr. Swinburne's *Tristram in Lyonesse*, and then to judge these poems from a mere comparison of three isolated quotations; such a judgment would probably be misleading, and certainly be worthless. And judgments formed on this method are more than ever worthless, when they are based upon descriptive selections, on "beautiful cameos of description ; " for, though it may seem a paradox at first sight, a description, which is attractive and striking in itself,

17

may in its connexion be an artistic and poetic blemish. The use of description in literature is a subtile and delicate thing, and the narrow limits of the writer's art are easily violated. A modern writer has every temptation to violate them; his own sentiment may incline him that way, and the public taste is quite certain to encourage him. Perhaps one of the chief benefits, which a modern author may gain from a constant reading of Dante and Homer, is to impress upon himself the severe way in which they avoid all direct and deliberate "word painting," all elaborate description; they recognize most perfectly the limitations of their art, and they are rewarded by making their scenes more vivid, their personages more distinct, than most other poets. Matthew Arnold is not a Dante or an Homer, in his matter he challenges no comparison with them; but in his manner, in his restrained severity of diction, he approaches the effect of the great ancients, and the great body of his work recalls their style.

Now, when we have come to some understanding with ourselves, as to whose manner precisely a certain poet recalls to us, we have gone a long way towards realizing that poet's value. Matthew Arnold says : " There can be no more useful help for discovering what poetry belongs to the class of the truly excellent, and can therefore do us most good, than to have always in one's mind lines and expressions of the great masters, and to apply them as a touchstone to other poetry. Of course we are not to require this other poetry to resemble them; it may be very dissimilar. But if we have any tact we shall find them, when we have lodged them well in our minds, an infallible touchstone for detecting the presence or absence of high poetic quality in all other poetry which we may place beside them. Short passages, even single lines, will serve our turn quite sufficiently. Take these two lines from Homer, the poet's

comment on Helen's mention of her
brothers :

"Ὣς φάτο· τοὺς δ' ἤδη κατέχεν φυσίζοος αἶα
Ἐν Λακεδαίμονι αὖθι, φίλῃ ἐν πατρίδι γαίῃ.

'So said she ; they long since in Earth's soft
                        arms were reposing,
There in their own dear land, their fatherland,
                        Lacedaemon.'

Take that incomparable line and a half
of Dante, Ugolino's tremendous words :

'Io non piangeva ; si dentro impietrai ;
Piangevan elli.'

'I wailed not, so of stone I grew within ;
They wailed.'

Take the lovely words of Beatrice to
Virgil :

'Io son fatta da Dio, sua mercè, tale,
Che la vostra miseria non mi tange,
Nè fiamma d'esto incendio non m'assale.'

'I am made such by God in his grace, that
your misery does not touch me, nor the flame of
this burning assail me.'

Take of Shakespeare a line or two of

Henry the Fourth's expostulation with sleep:

> 'Wilt thou upon the high and giddy mast
> Seal up the ship-boy's eyes, and rock his brains
> In cradle of the rude imperious surge?

Take of Milton that Miltonic passage:

> 'Darken'd so, yet shone
> Above them all the arch-angel; but his face
> Deep scars of thunder had intrench'd. and care
> Sat on his faded cheek.'

Add two such lines as:

> 'And courage never to submit or yield,
> And what is else not to be overcome:'

and finish with the exquisite close to the loss of Proserpine, the loss

> 'Which cost Ceres all that pain
> To seek her through the world.'

These few lines, if we have tact and can use them, are enough even of themselves to keep clear and sound our judgments about poetry, to save us from fallacious estimates of it, to conduct us to a real estimate.

" The specimens I have quoted differ widely from one another, but they have in common this : the possession of the very highest poetical quality. If we are thoroughly penetrated by their power, we shall find that we have acquired a sense enabling us, whatever poetry may be laid before us, to feel the degree in which a high poetical quality is present or wanting there. Critics give themselves great labour to draw out what in the abstract constitutes the characters of a high quality of poetry. It is much better simply to have recourse to concrete examples; to take specimens of poetry of the highest, the very highest quality, and to say : The characters of a high quality of poetry are what is expressed *there*. They are far better recognized by being felt in the verse of the master, than by being perused in the prose of the critic. Nevertheless, if we are urgently pressed to give some critical account of them, we may safely, perhaps, venture on laying down not indeed how

and why the characters arise, but where
and in what they arise. They are in
the matter and substance of the poetry,
and they are in it its manner and style.
Both of these, the substance and matter
on the one hand, the style and manner
on the other, have a mark, an accent, of
high beauty, worth, and power. But if
we are asked to define this mark and
accent in the abstract, our answer must
be : No, for we should be thereby dark-
ening the question, not clearing it, The
mark and accent are as given by the substance and matter of that poetry, and of
all other poetry which is akin to it in
quality."

It may be thought, perhaps, that all
this opposes what I have remarked, about
judging a poem as an whole, and about
not judging it from descriptive passages :
but these tests or touchstones of Matthew
Arnold's differ entirely from descriptive
passages, because they are of the very
essence of the poetry ; they are not fragments, which can be detached or inserted

without violating the artistic unity of
the poem, without, therefore, altering its
nature; and for this reason, they are satisfactory tests of its quality and style. And
the highest use of these tests does not
consist, as it appears to me, in choosing
lines however excellent, taken from poets
however famous, and applying them to
chance lines and passages of the author
whom we desire to estimate. Their highest value can only arise from our previous
knowledge of those poets, from whom we
choose them; and our application of
them should not be restricted to isolated
lines, and to single passages, here and
there. We must rather bear them in
mind, continually, as we go along; because they will keep the great masters
always before us, and they will oblige us
to judge the verse, which we are reading,
by the standard of their poetry.

The critic, I said, can discourse with
profit about the manner or style of a
poet. Now style is one of the most
baffling things in the world to define, or

to explain; there is only one thing more baffling, and that is, to attain it. But style can be felt profoundly by those who have the instinct for it: there can be no better test of style, than the test which Matthew Arnold gives; and if his own poetry be read with these test passages constantly in view, it will be found, I think, to recall the style and the manner of the great masters. Several of those passages, which I have already quoted from him appear to me to recall that style and that manner; but it is possible to choose lines which recall them even more vividly. Let us choose, as an example, these lines from *Sohrab and Rustum*:

"But Sohrab answer'd him in wrath: for now
The anguish of the deep-fix'd spear grew fierce,
And he desired to draw forth the steel,
And let his blood flow free, and so to die—
But first he would convince his stubborn foe;
And rising sternly on one arm he said:
'Man, who art thou who dost deny my words?
Truth sits upon the lips of dying men,
And falsehood, while I lived, was far from mine."

or these from *Tristram and Iseult*:

"The spirit of the woods was in her face;
She look'd so witching fair."

or these from *Urania*:

"His eyes be like the starry lights—
His voice like sounds of summer nights—
In all his lovely mien let pierce
  The magic of the universe!"

or these from *Isolation*:

"Yes! in the sea of life enisled,
  With echoing straits between us thrown,
Dotting the shoreless watery wild,
  We mortal millions live *alone*."

or these from the *Grande Chartreuse*:

"Our fathers water'd with their tears
This sea of time whereon we sail;
Their voices were in all men's ears
Who passed within their puissant hail.
Still the same ocean round us raves,
But we stand mute, and watch the waves."

or these from *Dover Beach*:

                "The sea of faith
Was once, too, at the full, and round earth's shore
Lay like the folds of a bright girdle furl'd;

But now I only hear
Its melancholy, long, withdrawing roar,
Retreating, to the breath
Of the night-wind, down the vast edges drear
And naked shingles of the world."

It is more convincing to take a few examples and compare them with test passages from the great masters, than to assert that Matthew Arnold's poetry has various abstract qualities of style, such as "restraint," severity," directness," or "simplicity." We can feel his manner in these examples, we have our experience of the manner and of the style of the great poets, and we can make our own comparison between their style and his. The comparison, will not, however, be fully satisfactory; we shall not realize all the value of Matthew Arnold's manner; until we have applied the test passages to other modern poets. We might apply them to Mr. Browning, for instance, as well as to Matthew Arnold; and then we shall perceive, that there is more than one way of resembling the

27

great masters We may apply them, also, to Lord Tennyson; and then we shall realize how subtile, and almost imperceptible, the resemblance can be. And if we apply them, finally, to Mr. Lewis Morris, we shall find how provoking critical rules are, and how, even though our intentions be scrupulously innocent, they may entangle us in the most distressing paradoxes; because, in this case, we shall be shown that a writer may have an enormous reputation, without resembling the great masters at all. I have already deprecated anything like passionate and partizan comparisons between contemporary poets, comparisons which are too absolute and hasty, which cannot be final; but a comparison of this indirect and impersonal nature may be of great assistance to a reader of modern poetry: it will help him to apply a common standard to the work of our contemporary poets, to regard their work from a fixed and definite point of view; it will restrain him from passionate and from partial judgments; it is the only method, which will enable him to overcome, or at least to restrain, his personal feelings, his private sympathies or tastes, and his individual caprice.

And if we pass from a poet's manner or style to his substance or matter, I believe, again, that a sounder judgment can be obtained by an indirect method of examination, by applying some fixed and classical standard to his poems; but, if we can get it, a poetical standard. It would be easy, and it would be in harmony with the usual practice of our reviewers, to take a certain number of Matthew Arnold's poems, and to declare that they have this or that aim and purpose; that they teach this lesson, or preach that doctrine. But this mode of judgment is arbitrary, inartistic, and exceedingly deceptive: "wide is the range of words! words may make this way or that way;" and if a wordy battle arise, who is to decide, which critic really understands the poet's lesson, or doctrine,

29

or purpose? And even though one of them should guess right, he has, surely, not done a fine thing because he has shown how to translate a poem into a sermon; that cannot be the right way to judge poetry. Voltaire says of a preacher, of course only in a romance: "Il devisa en plusieurs parties ce qui n'avait pas besoin d'être devisé; il prouva méthodiquement tout ce qui était clair; il enseigna tout ce qu'on savait. Il se ·passionna froidement, et sortit suant et hors d'haleine. Toute l'assemblée alors se réveilla, et crut avoir assisté a une instruction. Voîla un homme qui a fait de son mieux pour ennuyer deux ou trois cents de ces concitoyens!" The mutilation, the laborious proving of what is clear, the dismal teaching of what a single flash of right instinct, and that only, can reveal, are all familiar to the readers of sermonising critics, and to the congregations of literary preachers. These critics are less offensive, perhaps, than those "gushing" and unscholarly writers, who

30

drown the poets, and who display their ignorance, in a flood of verbiage; but they are far more tedious, and equally unprofitable. Matthew Arnold will again show us a better way of judging poetry. "We should conceive of poetry worthily," he says, "and more highly than it has been the custom to conceive of it. We should conceive of it as capable of higher uses, and called to higher destinies, than those which in general men have assigned to it hitherto. More and more mankind will discover that we have to turn to poetry to interpret life for us, to console us, to sustain us. Without poetry our science will appear incomplete, and most of what now passes with us for religion and philosophy will be replaced by poetry. Science, I say, will appear incomplete without it. For finely and truly does Wordsworth call poetry ' the impassioned expression of what is the countenance of all science; ' and what is a countenance without its expression? Again, Wordsworth finely and truly calls poetry 'the breath and finer spirit of all knowledge:' our religion, parading evidences such as those on which the popular mind relies now; our philosophy, pluming itself on its reasonings about causation and finite and infinite being; what are they but the shadows and dreams and false shows of knowledge? The day will come when we shall wonder at ourselves for having taken them seriously; and the more we perceive their hollowness, the more we shall prize 'the breath and finer spirit of knowledge' offered to us by poetry.

"But if we conceive thus highly of the destinies of poetry, we must also set our standard for poetry high, since poetry, to be capable of fulfilling such high destinies, must be poetry of a high order of excellence. We must accustom ourselves to a high standard and to a strict judgment. Sainte-Beuve relates that Napoleon one day said, when somebody was spoken of in his presence as a charlatan : ' Charlatan as much as you please ; but where is there *not* charlatanism ? ' ' Yes,' answers Sainte-Beuve, ' in politics, in the art of governing mankind, that is perhaps true. But in the order of thought, in art, the glory, the eternal honour is that charlatanism shall find no entrance ; herein lies the inviolableness of that noble portion of man's being.' It is admirably said, and let us hold fast to it. In poetry, which is thought and art in one, it is the glory, the eternal honour, that charlatanism shall find no entrance ; that this noble sphere be kept inviolate and inviolable, Charlatanism is for confusing or obliterating the distinctions between excellent and inferior, sound and unsound or only half-sound, true and untrue or only half-true. It is charlatanism, conscious or unconscious, when we obliterate these. And in poetry, more than anywhere else, it is unpermissible to confuse or obliterate them. For in poetry the distinction between excellent and inferior, sound and unsound or

33

only half-sound, true and untrue or only half-true, is of paramount importance. It is of paramount importance because of the high destinies of poetry. The best poetry is what we want; the best poetry will be found to have a power of forming, sustaining, and delighting us, as nothing else can. Constantly, in reading poetry, a sense for the best, the really excellent, and of the strength and joy to be drawn from it, should be present in our minds and should govern our estimate of what we read."

The function of the best poetry is, " to interpret life for us, to console us, to sustain us; " here, at any rate, a definite aim is placed before a serious reader of poetry; he is told, what to look for, when he is in search of good poetry. We can all understand the meaning of consolation and of support; we know quite well when we meet with a thing which " forms, delights, and sustains us." It is true, that we may fancy, now and then, we are "delighted" and "consoled" by poetry, with which we ought not to be pleased at all; we may " form " ourselves on models, which are deplorably vicious : but for that, there is no external remedy; we must acquire, each of us, our own experience, and we must grow into our taste! " The way to perfection is through a series of disgusts," as Mr. Pater admirably expresses it ; and, if we once set our face earnestly towards perfection, we shall soon meet with the disgusts, and marvel not a little that we ever admired them. As the only satisfactory method, when we wish to judge of a poet's manner, is to confront him with the great masters of style; so, in trying to form a judgment about his matter, it is equally indispensable to try to give the reader a test, which he can feel and experience. There can be no absolutely satisfying test except to read the poet's works, with a definite standard in mind, by which to compare them. " Who is able to infuse into me," Cardinal Newman asks, " or how shall I

35

imbibe, a sense of the peculiarities of the style of Cicero or Virgil, if I have not read their writings? " No one can infuse into a reader adequate ideas about an author, whom that reader has not read; although there is a fashionable school of criticism, which seems to imagine it can do this, and it tries to do it in the strangest way. It would be in the manner of that school to describe Matthew Arnold as an arum-lily; Mr. Browning, as a cactus in flower; and Lord Tennyson, as a sweet-pea: we all know the kind of discourse that would follow; it would not be about botany exactly, or about poetry exactly, but it would touch upon every subject that lies between the two. Though we should be fortunate, if the comparison were made between things of the same kind; for it is made more often between things which are not generally comparable with one another: the Parthenon, Wagner's music, the Divine Comedy, rainbows, the Crusades, and so on. All this may be effective, it is often elegant and pretty; but it is more adapted to reveal the ingenuity of the critic, than the work of that poet, whom it is his business to explain. "No description," says Cardinal Newman once more, "however complete, could convey to my mind an exact likeness of a tune, or an harmony, which I have never heard; and still less of a scent which I have never smelt; and if I said that Mozart's melodies were as a summer sky or as the breath of Zephyr, I should be better understood by those who knew Mozart than by those who did not." I would go still further than Cardinal Newman, because I believe that no description, however elaborate, could impress upon another mind the exact likeness of a scent or an harmony, even though he were familiar with the sound or smell described: and, for the same reason, no description and no comparison, even when the images are sane, apposite, and comparable with one another, can adequately express, either to an author

37

or to his readers, what he feels about a poet. If I were to compare a poet to a bird, a shell, or a star, my reader would get a very definite notion, but not of the poet; the definite notion conveyed to him would be, that my theory of criticism was unsound, and my practice insane. But if I say, that Matthew Arnold in his poetry seems to me, " to interpret life for us, to console us, to sustain us," and this in an eminent degree, those who have read him can test my opinion by their own experience; and those who have not read him will, at least, understand the kind of impression he makes upon me, and if they be familiar with poetry at all, they will be able to form some idea of Matthew Arnold's poetry; they will know to what sphere of poetry it belongs, with what sort of poetry it should be classed, with what order of poets he should be compared.

I said there were three things which the critic of a modern poet was able to discuss with profit: his manner, or style;

his matter, or substance; and that impression, which he makes upon a contemporary reader. We have discussed two of them, and at some length; because, in Cardinal Newman's words again, " when we assert, we do not argue." To assert, and to be believed without a shadow of additional proof, is the inalienable prerogative of a theologian. Not to assert, not even to argue, but to try and convince persuasively, is the business of a critic; and so, with a dread of bare assertion, and with a dislike of argument, I have endeavoured, in an indirect way, to ascertain the truth about the matter and the manner of the poet, whom we are now considering. And at last, perhaps, without incurring the charge of asserting too dogmatically, I may say what I feel about Matthew Arnold. In his style and in his manner he seems, to me, to recall the great masters; and this in a striking and in an abiding way. He recalls them in a striking way; because to recall them at

all is a rare gift, but to recall them
naturally and with no strained sense nor
jarring note of imitation, is a gift so exceedingly rare, that it is almost enough
in itself to place a writer among the
great masters, to proclaim that he is one
of them. To recall them in any way is
a rare gift, though not an unique gift;
a few other modern poets recall them
too; but with them, with everyone of
them, it is the exception when they resemble the great masters. They have
their own styles, which abide with them;
it is only now and then, by a flash of
genius, that they break through their
own styles and attain the one immortal
style. Just the contrary of this is true,
with Matthew Arnold: it is his own,
his usual, and his most natural style,
which recalls the great masters; and only
when he does not write like himself does
he cease to resemble them. It is Mr.
Swinburne who defines Matthew Arnold
as " the most efficient, the surest-footed
poet of our time, the most to be relied

on : " who says, that " what he does he is safest to do well ; " who asserts, that " more than any other he unites personality and perfection ; " and, that everywhere in his poetry " is the one ruling and royal quality of classic·work, an assured and equal excellence of touch." I only follow Mr. Swinburne, therefore, when I repeat, that Matthew Arnold resembles the great masters most, when he is most like himself; he is the most classical when he is most personal. If we consider the whole amount of his work, he seldom falls below himself; for " he is the surest-footed poet of our time ; " and, to return to prose, that is why I think Matthew Arnold resembles the great masters in an abiding way.

It is more difficult to speak of a poet's matter and substance, than of his style and manner. From the nature of his poetry, Matthew Arnold is to be numbered among the poets who " interpret life for us, who console and sustain us ; " but as to the degree in which he administers interpretation, comfort, and support, there may be a thousand opinions. So much will depend, for each reader, upon the stage of his own development when he first meets with a poet, and undergoes his influence; so much, again, will depend upon each reader's temperament. A great deal will depend, as well, upon our varying moods: at one time, a certain poet will be everything to us; at another time, he can give us nothing we want, he will be cold, valueless, and silent. There are, however, a few poets, who interpret life upon so many sides, that they can always give us something we want: poets of wide range, like Shakespeare, or Molière, or Sophocles; and there is Dante, who gives us a *New Life*, as well as a *Divine Comedy*. Poets of that order can appeal to every temperament, can satisfy every mood, can help us at every stage: they are for ever and ever; they " speak to time and to eternity." We hold them, therefore, to be supreme poets, and we place them

42

in an order apart; although we recognize, within that order, various degrees of worth and power. To this order, I do not think, that Matthew Arnold belongs; and, if I were asked for a reason, I should say it is chiefly because he fails to interpret that large and most engrossing element in man, which Dante interprets in his *New Life;* and just because he fails in the sphere of love and passion, his dramatic poems, although they contain fine things, are not great dramatically; they are too meditative and serene. This cannot be said of his narrative poems; they are, at any rate, brilliantly snccessful in their manner. But, what has been denied to Matthew Arnold in dramatic power, has been bestowed abundantly in personal power; in strenuousness, in concentration, in lucidity; and, therefore, his lyrical poems are exceedingly great. His lucidity and his concentration working upon his tender and emotional nature, and penetrated by his deep, his divine feeling of " the sense

43

of tears in mortal things," have made him greatest of all in his Elegies : his real strength is there, and some of his Elegies may rank with the greatest poems in that sort.

But I conceive that Matthew Arnold has a larger function than this, an higher sphere : his great style points to it ; the distinction and the potency of his work adapt him for it. Only a few months before he died, it was on the thirteenth of February, in 1888, Matthew Arnold gave an address, at Westminister, on Milton ; it was his last public discourse, and it was destined to be his first post-humous essay. He says : " In our race are thousands of readers, presently there will be millions, who know not a word of Greek and Latin, and will never learn those languages. If this host of readers are ever to gain any sense of the power and charm of the great poets of antiquity, their way to gain it is not through trans-lations of the ancients, but through the original poetry of Milton, who has the like power and charm, because he has the like great style.

" Through Milton they may gain it, for, in conclusion, Milton is English; this master in the great style of the ancients is English. All the Anglo-Saxon contagion, all the flood of Anglo-Saxon commonness, beats vainly against the great style, but cannot shake it, and has to accept its triumph! But it triumphs in Milton, in one of our own race, tongue, faith, and morals. Milton has made the great style no longer an exotic here; he has made it an inmate among us, a leaven, a power. Nevertheless, he and his hearers on both sides of the Atlantic are English, and will remain English :

' *Sermonem Ausonii patrium, moresque tenebunt.*'

" The English race overspreads the world, and at the same time the ideal of an excellence the most high and the most rare abides with it for ever."

I make no comparison here between

45

Milton and Matthew Arnold; but these
last words of his, about Milton, define
what I conceive to be his larger function.
No man, who attains to the great style,
can fail to have a distinguished function:
and Matthew Arnold, like Milton, will
be " a leaven and a power; " because he,
too, has made the great style current in
English. With his desire for culture
and for perfection, there is no destiny
he would prefer to this, for which his
nature, his training, and his sympathies,
all prepared him. To convey the message of those ancients, whom he loved
so well, in that English tongue, which
he was taught by them to use so perfectly, to serve as an eternal protest
against charlatanism and vulgarity, is
exactly the mission he would have chosen
for himself. But in this last speech of
his, he enunciates another truth, and we
cannot dwell too long upon it. In literature, in the things of the mind, by
which alone we truly live, political di-
visions do not count; whether we be

subjects or citizens, Americans, Australians, British, does not matter; we are all equally English, all equally concerned in the purity and in the power of our common language. Since it is an universal speech, its power is enormous; but, for this very reason, its purity may be the more endangered. The few writers of our language, therefore, who give us " an ideal of excellence the most high and the most rare," have an important function : we should study their works continually; and it should be a matter of passionate concern with us, that their "ideals;" that is, their definite and perfect models; should abide with us for ever.

In the meanwhile, and as long as this generation of ours is in possession of the earth, as long as its thoughts are current, Matthew Arnold will occupy an unique position; for he, and he alone in poetry, has given us modern thoughts in a classical form. A reader, who turns to him, will find the problems of our modern life, the troubles of our modern spirit, treated in a noble and a penetrating way, and in the great style. Such a reader will be calmed, consoled, braced; for Matthew Arnold " gives us so much to rest upon, so much which communicates his spirit and engages ours!" So winning and so abiding are these personal qualities in him, that many readers have imagined an old and intimate friend to be speaking to them; and this intimacy has tempted some of them, it may be, to overlook that power, that beauty, and that perfection, which are seldom absent from his writings. Other readers, it is evident, have been puzzled and offended by the " Distinction " of Arnold's work; by that rare quality, which is undeniable in him. Others, again, have been seduced, from the perfect clearness and simplicity of Mr. Arnold, by the miserable influences of this our day; by the more luxuriant though coarser styles, or by the louder though emptier tones, or by the imposing obscurity of its most fashionable names in prose and verse. "A test of great poetry," says a fine critic, whose English is a model to me, "is its abiding and unfailing power upon us, because of its indifference to time and place. A line of Virgil, written by the Bay of Naples, in some most private hour of meditation, all those long years ago! comes home to us, as though it were our own thought: upon each repetition, experience has made it more true and touching. Or, take some verse of Arnold, written at Oxford or in London, some few years past: it comes home to us as, though a thousand years had pondered it, and found it true.

> ' Tears
> Are in his eyes, and in his ears
> The murmur of a thousand years.'

And in beauty, in power of music and of phrase, the great poets are all contemporaries: an eternal beauty is upon the great works of art, as though they were from everlasting."

More and more, as the time goes on,

the world will acknowledge that Matthew
Arnold speaks thus to it, in the manner
and in the style of the great masters;
and his writing will take its true place
above the prettinesses, the affectations,
the eccentricities, which pass current on all
sides of us now, as great and genuine
poetry. And, in the still, cool atmosphere of the future, his voice will be
clearer and stronger, than it sounds to
us now, amid the heat and the noisy
personalities of our contemporary strife.
We who read him, and we who write
about him, will perish and pass away;
but he will remain, disengaged from all
that is low and temporary, a source of
strength and joy:

" But the majestic river floated on,
Out of the mist and hum of that low land,
Into the frosty starlight, and there moved,
Rejoicing."

It is only when we turn from verse to
prose that we can realize the full signifi-
cance of Matthew Arnold's loss. Now,
that he is gone, we are, all of us, ever so

much more at the mercy of stupidity
and of imposture and of vulgarity.
Who is there left, that can raise common
sense above the commonplace?   Who
can move practical things into the realm
of ideas, and handle them with distinction, with lightness, and with simplicity?
In prose, his loss is irreparable: in prose,
it is most melancholy to contemplate;
for " he furnished to others so much of
that which all live by," that he seemed
gifted with immortal youth, and destined
to criticise innumerable centuries with
that same keenness and buoyancy, which
he infused into this century of ours.
He gave us so much, that we could live
by, he understood so fully the life in
which he moved, that his departure is
like the visible passing away of the sanest
manifestation of the soul and intellect of
our generation.   *Nullum fere scribendi
genus non tetigit:*   It is in his prose
that we see the versatility of his mind,
and the width of his culture; but before
we can appreciate his work in prose, we

must try and realize what his aim was. He was a scholar, but not a pedant; he had no vain delusions about founding a school of thought, giving final opinions about things, establishing a system of criticism. Every one of these projects he abhorred, as detrimental to all fruitful thought, as the very delirium of mischievous vanity. " The old recipe, to think a little more and bustle a little less, seems to me still the best recipe to follow. So I take comfort when I find the *Guardian* reproaching me with having no influence; for I know what influence means, a party, practical proposals, action; and I say to myself: ' Even supposing I could get some followers, and assemble them, brimming with affectionate enthusiasm, in a committee room at some inn; what on earth should I say to them? what resolutions could I propose? I could only propose the old Socratic commonplace, *know thyself;* and how black they would all look at that!' " And so, when I hear him reproached because his writing, as people of a certain temper think, was not vigorous, or because his opinions were wanting in certainty: I reply, " no doubt it is as you say, but only raw and half educated people, like some divines and many journalists, are gifted with perfect certainty and undaunted vigour : they will always ' rush in where angels fear to tread.' " Matthew Arnold's attitude was rather " to try and approach truth on one side after another, not to strive nor cry, not to persist in pressing forward, on any side, with violence and self-will, it is only thus, it seems to me," he says, " that mortals may hope to gain any vision of the mysterious Goddess, whom we shall never see except in outline, and only thus even in outline. He who will do nothing but fight impetuously towards her or his own, one, favourite, particular line, is inevitably destined to run his head into the folds of the black robe in which she is wrapped." And so critics, with their heads enveloped in that

53

robe, have told us over and over again that " his politics were unpractical." A modern writer, himself a politician, confessed not long ago, that " Politics were a continual acceptance of the second best ; " and in saying this he, perhaps, flattered unduly the achievments of our politicians. But that saying accounts for Matthew Arnold's attitude towards politics ; it was his mission, he conceived, to indicate not what was brutally practical, what was most convenient, it may be, to party managers, but was ideally the best. " He brings thought to bear upon politics," as he says himself, of Burke, " he saturates politics with thought. I know nothing mor striking, and I must add that I know nothing un-English ; " and nothing which makes journalists and politicians more uncomfortable.

It was Matthew Arnold's fortune to make many people and many classes of people angry and uncomfortable ; he made them, as Dante expresses it,

"Guatar l'un l'altro, come al ver si guata," he made them look at one another, as men look when the truth is told them. He also made them feel towards him, as men too commonly feel towards the revealer of plain but disturbing and uncomfortable truths. Instead of feeling sorry for themselves at being wrong, they fly into a rage with that person who points out their evil state. As those lost souls, whom Dante celebrates, looked and felt towards him, so have the theologians, perhaps more often than any other class, looked and felt towards Matthew Arnold, though with how much justice I will not presume to decide. But Matthew Arnold says very truly, "the most characteristic thoughts one can quote from any writer are always his thoughts on matters of religion." And if we leave the theologians and the lost to gaze at one another, and turn ourselves to look simply at what Matthew Arnold says on these matters, we shall find many noble, and penetrating, and beautiful things : if we are wise we shall take thankfully those we can accept, and leave the remainder to those who have a taste for them.

After all, there are few modern writers who have more to give than Matthew Arnold, provided we realise exactly what it is he professes to give. He does not profess to give, I repeat, final opinions, or fixed systems, or dogmatic utterances. But he places things in the light of a clear and lucid intellect, he saturates them with thought, and brings a fresh current of ideas to bear upon them. He bids his readers examine their ingrained notions, and scrutinize their prejudices, and look at things as they really are, and judge them by an high standard of taste, of culture, and of intelligence. His influence is one of the finest intellectual disciplines, simply because he does not set up to be the master; he gives his readers, not rules, but flexibility of mind, and keenness of perception. About one thing only is he inflexible : he will accept no standard, but the highest and the noblest: nothing else will satisfy him, and no vain appearance of the best, however popular, or ingenious, or imposing, ever deludes ·him. This lofty tone has brought him numerous enemies: just as men get angry, when their faults are pointed out; and hate, not their errors, but their monitor : so, when their low ideals and their false tastes are exposed, they call the critic fastidious. Or they write a criticism on Matthew Arnold, and say that they find in him " so great a measure of delicate subtility that the atmosphere is generally more or less uncongenial." Very likely! for Matthew Arnold reveals everywhere that quality, which is uncongenial to all that is common; Distinction. " Of this quality the world is impatient : it chafes against it, rails at it, insults it, hates it ; it ends by receiving its influence and undergoing its law. This· quality at last inexorably corrects the world's blunders and fixes the world's ideals. It procures that the

popular poet shall not finally pass for a
Pindar, nor the popular historian for a
Tacitus, nor the popular preacher for a
Bossuet.''

I can only touch in the briefest way
upon Matthew Arnold's work in prose;
but how much could be said about prose,
now that we have so many rich and luxuriant masters of it flourishing on all
sides of us! I can only say, then, that
Matthew Arnold, in the manner and in
the style of his prose, give us the same
example as in his verse: the example of
the plain, simple, unpretentious style of
the masters of good prose; and his irony,
his humour, his fine breeding, place him
among the masters of the greatest prose.
That, which in verse is known as '' the
beautiful cameo of description,'' is known
in prose as '' the prose-poem.'' '' Qu'est
ce qu'un poème en prose,'' asks Voltaire,
'' sinon un aveu de son impuissance?''
'' What is a prose-poem but a thing
which testifies to its own and to its
author's impotence?'' I should reply,

" it certainly testifies to these; but it proclaims no less, that its author is ignorant of what prose should be." This age of ours makes many claims upon us, but none so unreasonable as when it bids us accept its mystifications for marvels, its tentative experiments for classical models, its experimental guesses for final truths; and so an healthy breeze of common sense from the eighteenth century is most invigorating for us now and then : for us, who live in an age which presumes to look down upon the great century of prose.

" Let us not bewilder our successors," says Matthew Arnold, in conclusion : " let us transmit to them the practice of poetry (and of prose) with its boundaries and wholesome regulative laws, under which excellent works may again, perhaps, at ·some future time be produced, not fallen into oblivion through our neglect, not yet condemned and cancelled by the influence of their eternal enemy, caprice. Sanity, that is the great virtue of the

59

ancient literature; the want of it is the great defect of the modern, in spite of all its variety and power." "Docile echoes of the eternal voice," he would say of the great masters in literature, " pliant organs of the infinite will, such workers are going along with the essential movement of the world." I always think that Matthew Arnold, as a prose writer, would wish the future to speak of him as one of the small band of workers who, in his own time and place, " echoed the eternal voice." He would like best to be known as a " pliant organ of the infinite will." That, it seems to me, was above all other things his aim in prose.

His aim in life, as he said not long ago, was " to be helpful to others, to be sympathetic : " and the affection of those, amongst whom he laboured, testifies to the noble and loving way in which he fulfilled this aim, during a long course of uncongenial employment, in which he was condemned by an hard fate, and by an harder generation, to wear away the precious years of his maturity. Those, who knew him, will not soon forget the charm of that gracious presence;

> " That comely face, that cluster'd brow,
> That cordial hand, that bearing free;
> I see them still, I see them now;
> Shall always see ! "

never can they forget the fascination and the happiness which were communicated by that buoyant though gentle spirit : the fifteenth of April shall come and shall go many times, before it cease to dawn upon a group of mourners, who are inconsolable.

June, 1888.

THE POETICAL WORKS ❦ OF MATTHEW ARNOLD

A Note upon Literature, considered as a Fine Art, and upon that practice and those theories of writing, which were in favour at one time among our Men of Letters.

NOT many days have passed, since a member was chosen by the French Academy. The accomplishments of this fortunate author were described by a newspaper, in one of its most ridiculous expressions, as being "*not far to seek*": after the search, it was discovered that "not one of Pierre Loti's books resembled anything previously written by any one else"; and this judgment was intended, neither as a rebuke to the Academy, nor as a satire upon the new Academician. Now there is a sense in which it is true, that every human being, who comes into the world, is different to the remainder of the species; and in this sense it is also true, that the writings of every human being are distinct and singular; but it was not in this broad way, that the newspaper spoke of Loti and of his productions; it was more enthusiastic for its hero, it was less cautious for itself; and it wished us to understand, that his works afforded new and unprecedented models in the art of writing. This was the amazing discovery, that was "*not far to seek:*" a fine discovery indeed, if it were true; and if it were possible, there could be no higher praise bestowed upon an author. But human nature being what it is, and the laws of thought and language being what they are, is it possible, we may ask, that the writings of any man should " resemble nothing previously written by any one else;" and, if it were possible, could those writings be pleasing or instructive? Were the same opinion expressed of any one's behaviour, we should imagine him to be either a primitive wild man, or an harmless disordered person out of Bedlam; and, if we pause and meditate, a like opinion will come to us about the exercise of every other human art or calling. What should we think of that painter, that merchant, that architect, that gardener, of whose operations, thoughts, and business it could be said, that they resembled nothing previously composed, imagined, or transacted, by any others of a similar employment? Some of the great architects and painters of this our day have, it is true, shown us productions, which resemble nothing fine, that was painted or built in former Ages; but it remains to be seen, whether Posterity will consider these productions to be works of genius, or works of eccentricity and pride. The truth is, every Art must be what our ancestors described as a Mystery; with its own fixed laws and constitution, with its own peculiar methods, and with its fine traditions. The novice, who would command the secrets of the Art, must first submit himself to a long apprenticeship, and to the most rigorous training; and his genius, if he be thus gifted, is to be shown, not by violating or by neglecting these wholesome and necessary laws, but by so mastering their principles as to extend them in a new direction, or to apply them in a more perfect way. If this be true in any one Art, surely it is true in all; and not less true, in the Art of writing.

> " Those rules of old, discover'd not devis'd,
> Are Nature still, but Nature methodiz'd:
> Nature, like Liberty, is but restrain'd
> By the same laws, which first Herself ordain'd.
> Nature to all things fix'd the limits fit,
> And wisely curb'd proud man's pretending wit."

In justice to Pierre Loti, however, it may be asserted that his admirer did him wrong when he said, that the manner of his composition was new and strange. " What chiefly moves us to admiration of Loti," says a more knowing critic, " is the very opposite quality; a precision and a lucidity, which give to his work the air of classical excellence. At a time when so much French prose is hideous with laboured phraseology, of science, of archaism, and of slang, Loti writes a ' pure and proper ' prose, simple and strong. Where Mr. Saintsbury sees artifice and affectation, we see a *curiosa felicitas;* that justifiable search for the right phrase, and the happy word, which only a good writer undertakes. In Loti's recent triumph over M. Zola, The Academy has shown, not its preference for extravagant beauty over extravagant ugliness; but for a beauty, which is classical and true. It is the author's admirable clearness, employed upon unfamiliar matters, which yields the effect of strangeness, and of deliberate novelty." Here we come upon a judgment, which is true, and therefore satisfying : Loti's originality is confessed; but, in praising him, the laws of his Art are neither contemned nor violated. "The first consideration for us is not whether we are amused and pleased by a work of art or mind, nor is it whether we are touched by it. What we seek above all to learn is, *whether we were right* in being amused with it, and in applauding it, and being moved by it."

It may be, that our modern authors and reviewers are all in a conspiracy to disguise their scholarship, as being out of fashion, and to dissemble the true extent of their accomplishments; but, in studying the large volume of their works, we do not seem to find in them a presiding and pervading scholarship, a perpetual recognition, that literature is a fine Art, and that they, the teachers and exponents of it, are the disciples of great masters, the students of great models, the guardians of an old tradition. The perception of this, I repeat, would seem to be as far from the thoughts and

68

methods, as from the works, of a large
number of our present authors and of
their critics : hence the apparent care-
lessness in the writings of the former,
and the more evident want of principle
in the judgments and opinions of the
latter. *In futilem quandam ac deformem
incidunt loquacitatem, qui, cum copiam
sint professi suam produnt inopiam; pari-
ter et rem obscurant, et miseras audit-
orum aures onerant.* Of this obscurity
and want of principle, the words about
Loti, with which I opened my disserta-
tion, are a fair example. Our critic in-
formed us, that his reasons were "*not
far to seek*," and they were not : for he
admitted and imprisoned the first wandering thought, that stole into the vacancy
of his mind, without reflection, without
considering whether his visitor were wise
or foolish ; and still less without pausing
to make any nice distinction, which might
explain or vindicate a sweeping and re-
volutionary judgment. " Not one of his
books resembles anything previously

written by any one else:" how purely ridiculous would this criticism be, were it not melancholy, that a professional judge of literature should bring himself to imagine such a fact possible, or such a judgment true. Nonsense is always foolish, and it may be irritating; but "*grand* nonsense," as Dr. Johnson has observed, "is insupportable." Every one of our reviewers should profit by the wisdom of that most cautious Frenchman, who was haunted by a perpetual fear, "La Peur d'être Dupe:" if he do not imitate this caution, he will be responsible, sooner or later, for the generation and birth of nonsense, perhaps of "*grand* nonsense." *Fortes creantur fortibus et bonis* is not always true in common life, though it is always true in literature; and, in literature, a foolish progeny may be attributed for certain to a foolish sire. But no author should rely upon nature's bounty, however good and strong his natural gifts may be; for in the delicate and learned Art of authorship, whether in the creative sphere of it or in the critical, the finest natural gifts do not exempt their owner from the obligation to read and study. "You can never be wise," Dr. Johnson observes again, "You can never be wise, unless you love réading:" and he says more forcibly in another place, "I never desire to converse with a man, who has written more than he has read." It is to be feared, therefore, that among certain of our modern authors Dr. Johnson would be reduced to silence : because, for want of reading, there is evolved by them, not literature, the result of scholarship and thought; but what Voltaire describes better as "les excréments de la littérature;" evolved, that is, by the writer's own internal operations, like a spider's web.

"Who shames a scribbler? break one cobweb thro';
He spins the slight, self-pleasing thread anew :
Destroy his fib, or sophistry, in vain ;
The creature's at his dirty work again,
Thron'd on the centre of his thin designs,
Proud of a vast extent of flimsy lines."

"Proud of a vast extent of flimsy lines" is not so bad a description of our current literature, taken in the mass, or of the disposition of its manufacturers. My comparison of it, to a spider's web, might be justified on several grounds; but one reason for the justice of it "*is not far to seek*," and this reason will show how far were our great authors from desiring to produce books, which "resembled nothing previously written by any one else:" for they desired to produce literature, not to throw off the excrements of authorship. As we examine the lives of our men of letters, we find that in every Age, they set before themselves some particular models; the study of which was their business, and their delight, which they gloried in trying to reproduce; not slavishly nor pedantically, but liberally, in the manner of true genius, and according to the fine laws and traditions of the art of writing. In the first place, there were the Greek and Roman authors; in whose works

72

our old writers were trained religiously, whom they never ceased to frequent, to enjoy, and to revere. They would one and all have supplicated the Ancients, in the words of Pope :

" O may some spark of your celestial fire
The last, the meanest, of your sons inspire ;
(That on weak wings, from far, pursues your flights ;
Glows while he reads, but trembles as he writes)
To teach vain wits a science little known,
T' admire superior sense, and doubt their own."

But in addition to these, the necessary teachers of all who would practise writing as an art, our own great masters chose deliberately to inform themselves upon some later model. In Chaucer, there is what Primers and Guide Books, those *clysters* for dyspeptic students, describe as his French manner, and as his Italian manner : by the latter expression we are to understand, that he was a most reverent admirer of Dante and Boccaccio ; that is to say, he studied the best modern literature he could find ; and without depreciating his native genius, we may

73

assert that he and his works were much the better for these liberal pursuits. Spenser, again, was no less diligent in cultivating the Italians. I will not enter upon the vexed question of Shakespeare's reading, except to affirm that it was wide: I only touch upon Ben Jonson's learning, which is even squandered upon the surface of his prose; and thus we pass through the other dramatists, all very much "Italianate," to Milton. In his pages, the classical authors meet us at every turn: but we find in Milton, besides a loving intimacy with the classics, and with the great Italians, an acknowledgement of his obligations to his two English predecessors. After recording his admiration for Chaucer, he says of Spenser,

> "And if aught else great bards beside
> In sage and solemn tunes have sung,
> Of turneys and of trophies hung,
> Of forests, and enchantments drear,
> Where more is meant than meets the ear."

Milton thus finely inaugurates that

venerable tradition of English letters, by which Spenser is enthroned as "the poets' poet." And so the fair inheritance of learning was transmitted, from Milton to Dryden, from Dryden to Addison, to Pope, to Johnson: the taste and the models of these authors changing, their devotion to scholarship unchanged. *Forsitan et nostrum nomen miscebitur illis,"* was the pious wish of Johnson, as he mused with Goldsmith in the Poets' Corner; and the words express his constant attitude towards the great authors of the past. Nor did our Augustan writers hesitate to confess their obligations to Boileau, and to the severe models of the French. The fashion is, to chatter about the immorality of France: to purse the lips and look unutterable things over the wickedness of the French authors; over the lewdness of Boileau and Corneille, that is, of Racine, of Bossuet, of Fénelon; for these, being the great models at that time in their own country, were after all the masters whose teaching was supreme in ours. To talk of their immorality would be mere cant, with which Art and Letters would have no concern, though the charge were true. It is not only truer, but more profitable, I think, to consider the severity of those great writers, both in their matter and in their style; and to realize, that, without their strait example, we might have had neither an Augustan Age of English prose, nor the polite and finished literature of the Eighteenth Century. :

"We conquer'd France, but felt our captive's charms,
Her arts victorious triumph'd o'er our arms ;
Britain to soft refinements less a foe,
Wit grew polite, and numbers learn'd to flow."

"A man, who has not been to Italy, is always conscious of an inferiority ; " and a nation, we may add, that has not been to school in Italy, is always inferior in its Art and in its Literature. If we examine the English literature before Chaucer's time, and after it, we shall realise what Italian influence can do; the one great master, who came among us before the middle of the sixteenth century, was trained by the Italians. This is not the place to speak at large of the influence of Italy upon English Art: I wish only to record, in passing, how much our language owes to the great masters of Italy and France:

" Still do thy sleepless ministers move on ",

we may say of Art, as well as of Nature; and thus the treasures of civility and language are circulated through the human family.

"Language is the Sacred Fire in this Temple of Humanity," says Coleridge, "and the Muses are its especial and Vestal Priestesses." The phrase is magnificent, the illustration happy; they vindicate the high office of Art and Letters; they remind us, that the altar of knowledge must be served continually by a succession of initiated ministers, the acolytes and bedes-men of the Muses'

ritual.   It is not necessary to pursue the
investigation ; to show that all our great
authors were not only men of parts, but
men of reading . not one of them learned,
perhaps, not Gray, not Milton, as Bentley
or Scaliger was learned : that kind of
learning in excess may be a dangerous
accomplishment in a man of letters ; " a
mere antiquarian is a rugged being ; "
but they were familiar with books, and
proficient in the Art of authorship ; they
were learned, that is, in the liberal way,
if not in the high degree, of Erasmus.
Of him it hath been written eloquently,
by an old French translator of *The
Praise of Folly*, " Erasme fut d'une vaste
Litérature, & d'un discernement exquis :
il possédoit à fond les Auteurs ; & per-
sonne n'a peut-être, jamais si bien mis
en oeuvre le savoir & l'érudition.   Il
excelloit dans la connoissance des Livres ;
& le principal but de son assiduité à
l'étude, étoit de réfléchir sur les moeurs."
The literature of Erasmus, that is to
say, was " at bottom a criticism of life : "

78

but it owed all its unequalled fineness and power to its author's happy intercourse with the ancient writers; to his firm persuation that writing is an Art; to his acquaintance with the models of that art, and to his perfect mastery of its laws, of its methods, and of its tradition. It may be thought a compliment by a modern critic, to say of an author, that " not one of his books resembles anything previously written by any one else: " Erasmus would have thought otherwise; he would have said to our critic, and to many critics, *Dicat igitur suae quisque linguae quoties rapitnr ad loquendum: Lingua quo vadis? utrum prodesse paras, an laedere?* The familiars of Erasmus have " *not far to seek,*" if they would know how that great wit and scholar were likely to accept a dubious compliment, or into what place he would have sent its maker.

But it was not our great authors alone, who were men of reading; I contend that our little authors, the minor poets,

79

the smaller critics, were also men of
reading in their various degree; and that
they, too, held sound views about literature, as an Art, as a tradition. Let us
examine the little authors of any period;
the courtiers of Henry VIII. and of
Elizabeth, " the wits of either Charles's
days," the witlings of Queen Anne or
of the early Georges; think as we may
about their work, about its pedantry or
its euphuism, about its conceits, about
its "artificiality," whatever that may
mean, we can trace in it a deliberate
effort to be scholarly, and to practise
Letters as an Art. The works of all
those periods were based on scholarship,
they were formed upon some definite
plan or school, they rested upon what I
call tradition : whereas the great quantity
of the minor verse and criticism of to-
day seems to be inspired by nothing but
emotion, to be formed upon no models,
and to rest upon nothing more stable
than the transient feelings of its authors,
who themselves appear to have no notion

80

that literature must be viewed, acquired, and practised, like any other of the arts. It seems to me, that in this difference of attitude and of practice, we find some explanation of the present barbarity and wildness of our minor verse and criticism. If a man will be a painter, he must learn to draw; no easy accomplishment, as I am told. He must be at the pains to master his anatomy and his perspective. Then, having learnt and practised the rudiments of his Art, he must frequent the great masters of it; he must meditate their works, and copy them. If he would be a true scholar, he will read their lives; he will dwell with them; he will possess their thoughts and breathe their atmosphere. In addition, he will try to know what they and other skilful persons have recorded about the theory and the practice of his Art: and when he has done this, he will find that he has wandered into the broad and shining fields of literature. So it is with the Art of Painting: so it was with the Art of

Writing. But this is the age of Primers, of Examinations, and of easy ways to knowledge. If the end of education were to gather facts, nothing could be better than a summary; but the Art of Writing may not be acquired, nor taught, in this barbarous and hurried manner. It was not thus, that the old authors were exercised in literature. " Burke had always a ragged Delphin *Virgil* not far from his elbow." The old authors, in other words, frequented the great masters of their Art, they breathed their atmosphere, and we can see the bounteous effect of it throughout their writings; but, if we may judge from modern writings, this is just what modern authors neglect to do, and we can see the effects of their negligence in the incivility of their pages. How could he ever paint, who, instead of frequenting the galleries, should study imperfect reproductions from the paintings in them; a hand from one, a vestment from another, a cloud or a prospect from a third, but

82

nothing as an whole, Instead of possess-
ing the mind of Rubens, our student
would be content to know, that he was
born in one year and died in another,
that he married, that he lived in splendour
and was something of a public man. To
know this, is good ; but the knowledge
will not teach you how to paint, nor will
a like knowledge about Addison teach
you how to write. This kind of education would be perceived at once to be
ridiculous for a painter : yet, with our
Primers and Selections, this is precisely
the education, which we provide in this
our day for a student of literature, for
an intending writer ; and the attitude of
mind, which tolerates this way of education, is more sad to contemplate than the
literature it produces. Of how many
such wasted students must we own, as
Johnson owned with truth of Voltaire,
Vir est acerrimi ingenii; of how many
more must we add, as Johnson added
with less truth, *Vir est paucarum liter-
arum?* Not all the gifts of Voltaire

can produce good literature, nor all the
gifts of Mantegna good painting, without study and without practice; without
some rational theory about their several
Arts, and some familiarity with the great
masters in them. He who has emotions,
but not genius, and much zeal, but little
training, can only hope at best " to be
dull in a new way and therefore to be
great." His books will be unscholarly
and monstrous, a shame, and not an or-
nament, to Art and Letters; and of them
it may be said with truth, in some low
sense, that " they resemble nothing previously written by any one else: " such
an author will be worthy of our critic,
and of his amazing discovery; and, by
learned persons, the reasons for his de-
ficiency will never be "*far to seek*." For
the purposes of Art, it were better to
know one book of Horace and a few
essays by Addison or Goldsmith, than to
master the facts and dates in all our Primers. *Non multa sed multum*, is the true
way in literature: it is well to know

84

something of " The Hundred Best Books ; " it is indispensable for an author to be familiar with the half dozen, which are for him the best, to dwell with them, to handle them continually.

But I would not leave my reader with the impression, that the minor literature of old was all good, and the minor literature of to-day all bad. What I say is, that the old writers, taking the general average of them, had a different conception of literature from ours; they practised and studied it in a different manner: it is this difference of attitude, upon which I would lay stress, rather than the difference between their literature and the literature of to-day. That they could be bad enough, we have their own works and the witness of *The Dunciad* to prove : perhaps I can distinguish best by saying, that where they are bad, we are mad; at any rate, there was more method in the madness of those dunces. They had too much education for their wits ; we bestow too little training upon our emotion. Let us hear an old critic, long since forgotten, who wrote thus of Pope's *Essay on Criticism*: "His precepts are false or trivial, or both; his thoughts are crude and abortive; his expressions absurd, his numbers harsh and unmusical, his rhymes trivial and common. Instead of majesty, we have something that is very mean; instead of gravity, something that is very boyish; instead of perspicuity and lucid order, we have but too often obscurity and confusion." Whatever we may think of this judgment, we must own that the critic had something definite to say, and that he knew very well how to say it, and how to punctuate it. Training can but direct and improve a judgment; it cannot give one: here we have a bad judgment expressed in the terms of good literature; if I must choose between two sorts of mediocrity, I prefer this to a mad judgment in words unscholarly and loose. Now I will take a good author of to-day, whose works are a striking illustration of what I wish to prove. Every one, who has a true taste for literature, must delight in the poetry of Mr. Austin Dobson; in whom he will meet with all the finer qualities, which he admires in the most polished authors. The exquisite verses of Mr. Dobson inform his readers that Horace is never "far from his elbow;" and that he has conversed familiarly with the polite scholars of the last Age, both among ourselves and among the French. We cannot but see in him, that he has been a disciple of great masters, a student of great models, that he considers himself to be the guardian of a fine tradition. He has practised literature, as an Art: he has, and will have, an artist's high reward.

There are many writers, more practised than I shall ever be, who have discoursed on style; of that vexed question I do not wish to speak: but Mr. Austin Dobson has reminded me of the excelcent way in which the great writers of the last Age pursued their Art; and I wish to say something about that, now we have examined their attitude towards the Art itself. I wish to draw attention to their correct vocabulary, to their bold and pregnant language, and to their scholarly punctuation. Among our present authors, the art of punctuation is a lost accomplishment; and it is usual now to find writings with hardly anything but full stops: colons and semi-colons are almost obsolete; commas are neglected, or misused; and our slovenly pages are strewn with dashes, the last resources of an untidy thinker, the certain witnesses to a careless and unfinished sentence. How different, and how superior, is the way of the great authors of the eighteenth century; who, though they can be homely and familiar, never lay aside the good breeding and the civility of a polished Age. In their writings, the leading clauses of a sentence are distinguished by their colons: the minor clauses, by their semi-colons; the nice meaning of their detail is expressed, the pleasure and convenience of their readers are alike increased, by their elegant and proper use of commas. The comma, with us, is used as a loop or bracket, and for little else : by the more accurate scholars of the last Age, it was employed to indicate a finer meaning ; to mark an emphasis, an inversion, or an elision ; to introduce a relative clause ; to bring out the value of an happy phrase, or the pretty meaning of an epithet. And thus the authors of the great century of prose, that orderly and spacious time, assembled their words, arranged their sentences, and marshalled them into careful periods : without any diminution from the subtile meaning of their thought, or any sacrifice of their directness and their vigour, they exposed their subject in a dignified procession of stately paragraphs ; and when the end is reached, we look back upon a perfect specimen of the writer's Art. We have grown careless about form, we have little sense for balance and proportion, and we have sacrificed the good manners of literature to an ill-bred liking for haste and noise : it has been decided, that the old way of writing is cumbersome and slow ; as well might some guerilla chieftain have announced to his fellow barbarians, that Caesar's legions were not swift and beautiful in their manoeuvres, nor irresistible in their advance. I have spoken of our straggling phrases, with nothing but full stops, or with here and there a solitary and bewildered comma : they are variegated, upon our disordered pages, with shorter sentences, sometimes of two words. This way of writing is common in Lord Macaulay, or in the histories of Mr. Green; and I have found it recommended, as an elegant device, in Manuals and Primers. With the jolting and disconnected fragments of these authorities, I would contrast the musical and flowing periods of Johnson's *Poets*, or the easy progress of an Addisonian discourse.

Dr. Birkbeck Hill, in the delightful

Preface to his *Boswell*, explains how he was turned by an happy chance to the literature of the eighteenth century ; and how he was tempted to read on and on in the enchanting pages of " *The Spectator.*" " From Addison in the course of time I passed on," he continues, "to the other great writers of his and the succeeding age, finding in their exquisitely clear style, their admirable common sense, and their freedom from all the tricks of affectation, a delightful contrast to so many of the eminent authors of our own time." There is no one fit to study literature, who is not impressed by the common sense and the clear style of the eighteenth century ; and the more he is impressed, the more will he resent the too frequent absense of sense and clearness, from a large number of the eminent authors of the nineteenth century. In Mr. Ward's selection from the English Poets, there may be read, side by side, a notice of Collins and of Gray : the first, by Mr. Swinburne ; the other, by Mr. Matthew

Arnold. The essay upon Gray is quiet in tone, it has an unity of treatment and never deserts the principal subject; it is suffused with light, and is full of the most delicate allusions. The essay upon Collins, by being written in superlatives and vague similes, deafens and perplexes the reader; and the author, by squandering his resourses, has no power to make fine distinctions, nor to exalt one part of his thesis above another.

Non cuivis homini contingit adire Corinthum.

The old writers were more restrained in their utterances, and therefore they could be more discriminating in their judgments; they could be emphatic without noise and deep without obscurity, ornamental but not gairish, carefully arranged, but not stiff nor artificial. They exhibit the three indispensable gifts of fine authorship, the natural reward of Letters as an Art: *simplicitas munditiae, lucidus ordo, curiosa felicitas.* Then, how

tender were the consciences of these fine
scholars towards the smallest questions of
their Art : Boswell, in recording one of
Dr. Johnson's speeches about the Papists,
printed the word *laceration* in italics ; because it was a term of surgery, it was not
properly a term to use in literature. For
a similar reason, I too have printed the
ridiculous expression " *not far to seek* " in
italic letters ; and that would be the better
way of printing our critic's wonderful
discovery, his dubious compliment to
the unfortunate Loti, that " not one of
his books resembles anything previously
written by any one else." And now we
take our leave of this wandering thought,
of this foolish and perfidious visitor,
who stole into our critic's mind, and
debauched his judgment. We have con-
fronted him with the theories and with
the practice of the great masters in the
Art of writing, and we have brought
him out into the healthy light and air of
the Eighteenth Century : how ridiculous
doth he now appear, as he stands thus

exposed before us, all brazen-faced and silly.

Spectatum admissi, risum teneatis, amici ?

Pope has told us that the last and greatest art for an author is "the art to blot :" M. Renan, one of the most distinguished masters of writing in this Age, has said, that it is the art of making transitions, of passing imperceptibly and naturally from one subject to another. The newspapers are fond of doing this in one more of their improper phrases, the twin brother of their expression, "*it is not far to seek* ;" and therefore a phrase to distinguish by italics, and to avoid. "*It is a far cry*," they will inform you, when they can join two irrelevant subjects by no other artifice ; and I might elude my difficulty, and delude my reader, by saying "*it is a far cry*" from the Eighteenth Century to Mr. Matthew Arnold. But I have introduced this low phrase to expose it, not to use it ; and I will enter upon the second portion of my subject in a better way. "The criticism which, throughout Europe, is at the present day meant, when so much stress is laid on the importance of criticism and the critical spirit, is a criticism which regards Europe as being, for intellectual and spiritual purposes, one great confederation, bound to a joint action and working to a common result; and whose members have for their common outfit, a knowledge of Greek, Roman, and Eastern antiquity, and of one another." This is Mr. Arnold's definition of that science in which he is an acknowledged master, the science of criticism: his words show, how large and rigorous a demand he made upon the profession of an author; and, if we add to this another of his definitions, that culture is knowing the best that has been thought and written in the world, we shall find ourselves once more considering those views of the Art of Writing, which we saw the great masters held. We followed their tradition, in English literature, until we

MATTHEW ARNOLD

found ourselves in the company of Pope
and Johnson; and now, after more than
a century has elapsed, another great
master in the Art of Writing has precisely the same thing to say to us, both
in his exhortations and in his models.

"The thing that hath been, it is that
which shall be; and that which is done,
is that which shall be done: and there is
no new thing under the sun. Is there
anything whereof it may be said, See,
this is new? it hath already been of old
time, which was before us." This is a
better text, I think, to introduce us to a
great writer, than the words with which
our unknown critic chose to introduce
us to the works of Pierre Loti; at any
rate, it is not a libel upon the subject of
my discourse. It was my privilege, some
three years ago, to speak of Mr. Arnold's
poetry; and after that lapse of time,
there is nothing I can wish unsaid, but
nothing either, that I can well repeat. I
had then the melancholy office to speak
of Mr. Arnold's death, and to review

his writings : I have now the easier and pleasanter duty to notice a new edition of his poems. These have been collected into one volume, of which the first impression was consumed immediately. In a letter, which was published in *The Hobby Horse*, Mr. Arnold spoke of himself as " a less than half popular author ; " and he said again, " I never have been broadly popular, and I cannot easily bring myself to believe I shall ever become so : " he would, therefore, have been very pleased with the reception of his book ; and the second edition, as I hope, has given place to others already. Mr. Arnold's collected poetry forms one small volume ; and there is nothing new in it, except the early, unfinished poem, which he contributed to *The Hobby Horse*. Nothing has been added, which he would not have included himself ; and his own order, his own arrangement of of the poems, has been preserved : in both of these respects, I hope all future editors will be as careful of his wishes.

97

But there is one change, that I should like to see; not so much a change, as an addition: an addition, which might perhaps be made now, which it may be impossible to make if this opportunity be lost. Without altering the present order of the poems, I should like, if it be possible, to have the date assigned to each of them.

"We must confess the faults of our favourite, to gain credit to our praise of his excellence. He that claims, either in himself or for another, the honours of perfection, will surely injure the reputation which he desires to assist." The time has not come for estimating Mr. Arnold's work: but I, much as I admire him, have never contended that he is faultless; what I do say is, that his faults are occasional and few, his excellencies continual and many. "If I come to an orchard, and say there's no fruit here, and then comes a poring man, who finds two apples and three pears, and tells me, 'Sir, you are mistaken, I have found

98

both apples and pears,' I should laugh
at him : what would that be to the purpose ? " And I think when the worst
has been said, that Mr. Arnold's ad-
mirers may still have the laugh against
the " poring man," and his collection of
blemishes.

There is a Latin verse, I think by
grave Tibullus, which always seems to
me in its propriety to express very well
the singular, but easy, refinement of Mr.
Arnold :

Mille habet ornatus mille decenter habet.

If it require a " poring man " to collect
Mr. Arnold's blemishes, it would require
a " poring man," too, to collect what it
used to be the fashion to describe as his
" beauties " ; what the present fashions
would call his " striking passages," his
" cameos of description." In this general
and quiet excellence is his highest praise,
among true judges of poetry ; it is in
the possession of it, that he most nearly
resembles the great masters, and is a

worthy representative of those traditions of good literature, which we have been considering. And what, it may be asked, is the end of all this hard training, of this austere tradition of yours, of the infinite labour of those, you call the great masters in literature; what, in short, is the end of your Art of Writing? To that question, there might be several answers: I might say, that he, who asks it, does not deserve to know; that by the very fact of asking it, he proves that he can never know. But, if I might answer shortly and imperfectly, I would say: the end of the Art of Writing is to give pleasure, and to satisfy as many as possible of our highest faculties. "Works of imagination excel by their allurement and delight; by their power of attracting and detaining the attention. That book is good in vain, which the reader throws away. He only is the master, who keeps the mind in a pleasing captivity; whose pages are perused with eagerness, and in hope of new pleasure are perused again;

and whose conclusion is perceived with an eye of sorrow, such as the traveller casts upon departing day."

July: 1891.

SOME LETTERS OF MATTHEW ARNOLD.

HE second anniversary of Mr. Arnold's death will fall soon after the publication of our April number, which is adorned with a poem about his grave at Laleham : Mr. Arnold was an indulgent reader of our magazine, even in the days of its wayward and inexperienced youth ; he read its maturer productions with constant sympathy and approval ; he was always interested in the fortunes of the *Hobby Horse* ; and, to assist its fortunes, he was obliging enough to become a contributor himself. Alike for the pleasure of my readers, and that they might join with me in

103

celebrating the fifteenth of April, more
tenderly, and with a more intimate sense
of our irreparable loss, I have desired,
for some time, to let them share with
me in a few of Mr. Arnold's letters;
especially in some of those which refer
to the *Hobby Horse*; and now, through
Mrs. Arnold's kindness, I am enabled to
realize my desire: I leave the letters to
tell their own story; adding, here and
there, a sufficient explanation; and I
have inserted a fac-simile from the manuscript of the poem, which Mr. Arnold
gave to me for our July number, in
1887.*

The first letter, which I desire to pub-
lish, refers to some poems in one of our
earliest numbers; the reference is most
interesting, because it enunciates Mr.
Arnold's belief, that poetry should be
simple, direct, and plain: it was the
theory of the great poets; but not the
theory, as it would seem, and certainly
not the practice, of the more illustrious

* Omitted here.

writers of verse, in the present day. I had written to Mr. Arnold from Italy; and I had sent him some ivy from the grave of " Thyrsis." The dogs, whom he mentions, are two dachs hounds, Port and Hock; a representation of Port, which is both decorative and accurate, is given as the tailpiece to this article.*

Cobham, Surrey. Jan. 1st, 1886.
My dear Galton,
I have been abroad for some time on a school-errand from the Governmnet; and on my return I find your letter, verses, and ivy—also the charming photographs of the two dogs. We ourselves have two, and that must suffice us; but if we outlive either of them, his place could not be better filled than by a child of your fascinating Pair.
The merit of the verses is in the firm effort to have and express a definite meaning. I like best the Mercury Sonnet because this effort is there, perhaps, most successful. It

* Omitted here.

105.

would have been more entirely successful still, to my thinking, if you had brought out on what errands *you conceived Mercury as visiting both the Under-World and this World of ours. Exercise in verse cannot but be valuable to you if you set yourself to be thus distinct; and if you can really succeed in being distinct, with your serious purpose and command of language, you are sure to interest others.*

I wish you a happy New Year : I am returning to the Continent almost immediately and shall then have to face a second expedition to America; after that, I hope to have a quiet time, but at present this seems very far off.

Ever yours truly, Matthew Arnold.

Stockbridge, Mass. July 30th, 1886. *My dear Galton,*
The best thing I can do here for the Magazine (in which I am interested for Image's sake as well as yours) is to get my son-in-law to lay it upon the table of the University Club in New York, the best

*centre that I know of for the kind of people
likely to be interested in such a publication.
What you have written about Assisi is
full of interest, but for the general public
it should have perhaps had more about
Assisi itself; although the questions of
criticism treated in the middle and latter
part of the paper are in themselves highly
important, and you have treated them with
judgment and insight.*

*This climate does not suit me; and, as
as far as health and efficiency are concerned,
I shall be very glad to be back in England
again. I hope to find the state of Nab
Scar less afflicting than you say.*

Ever truly yours, Matthew Arnold.

I had written to Mr. Arnold from
Windermere: his letter refers to the
July *Hobby Horse*, for 1886; and, in the
summer of that year, the Manchester
water works were being carried through
the Rydal valley, at the back of Wordsworth's house, and above his favourite
walk.

The next letter refers to a Sonnet on Marcus Aurelius, published in the *Hobby Horse* for April, 1887.

Cobham, Surrey. Decr. 16th, 1886.
My dear Galton,
I like the Sonnet, and the man who inspires it is indeed excellent reading. I have a political article to write which I would fain write in his sense as much as possible: but I know, if I begin to re-read him, I shall go on and on and leave the promised political article unbegun.
We all send sympathy to Port—affectionate sympathy.
Ever yours sincreely, Matthew Arnold.

Pains Hill Cottage,
Cobham, Surrey. Jan. 13th, 1887.
My dear Galton,
When I take up the " Hobby Horse "
to look at it, I find myself going right through it; it has so much merit that its restricted publicity is really to be lamented.
108

Could not something be done? What you say of Symonds is true and good.

> *Ever yours, Matthew Arnold.*

I am sorry Port is amiss.

The mention of Mr. Symonds refers to a notice of his *Catholic Reaction*, the last part of his collected materials for an history of *The Renaissance in Italy*. A month or two after receiving this letter, I wrote to Mr. Arnold, to ask him whether the " something to be done " might not include a contribution from himself; and to tell him, that Mr. Ruskin had given us an article.

> *Hastings. April* 21*st*, 1887.

My dear Galton,

Your letter has been forwarded to me here, where I have come to try and get rid of a sharp attack of lumbago. I shall find the " Hobby Horse," no doubt, on my return home.

I do not like to undertake anything as to contributing, for I have promised as much as I can well perform for this year. But if I can make anything of a little Horatian Echo, in verse, which has lain by me for years, discarded because of an unsatisfactory stanza, you shall have it. But I repeat that I can promise *nothing.*

I shall be curious to see what Ruskin has done for you. His is indeed a popular influence; I will not say that a contribution from me would do you no service; but it is not to be compared, as a help with the great public, to one from J. Ruskin.

Hard dry winds, and an aching back! but the sea is always inspiriting.

Ever truly yours, Matthew Arnold.

In the spring of 1887, I wrote an essay upon Thomas Cromwell; and I asked Mr. Arnold, whether I might dedicate my volume to him.

Pains Hill Cottage,
          Cobham. April 7th, 1887.
My dear Galton,
I liked your paper in " Macmillan."

You have an excellent subject in Thomas Cromwell: it shows how ignorant I am, that when my wife said he was Lord Essex, I contradicted her—but she proved to be quite right. Do you not think that your dedication is a little strong, applied to one who could make such a blunder about your subject? I do, but I will not interfere with your freedom of action, if I have been of use to you and you wish to say so. We have a raging north wind here, and no flowers yet. We have just lost our dear dear mongrel, Kaiser, and we are very sad.

Ever truly yours, Matthew Arnold.

As soon as I heard of Mr. Arnold's bereavement I offered him another dachs hound, Hans, about whom I have several letters, and who is mentioned again in this series. Kaiser died upon the sixth of April; and he was commemorated, in the following July, in an Elegiac Poem. The next letter refers to a box of fritil-

laries; Oxford fritillaries, consecrated to
"Thyrsis" and to Matthew Arnold's
"pastoral song."

Cobham.   May 6th, 1887.
My dear Galton,
    You could not have sent me a prettier
and pleasanter present. The purple flowers
are come out to-day, and I think the white
ones will come out to-morrow. They are
all beautiful.
            Ever truly yours, Matthew Arnold.
    You shall hear about Hans as soon as
quarters are prepared for him.

Cobham, Surrey.   June 4th, 1887.
My dear Galton,
    I send you the thing I promised—a relic
of youth.   It is quite artificial in sentiment,
but has some tolerable lines, perhaps.   Let
me see a proof of the lines, and believe me,
most truly yours,   Matthew Arnold.

The poem is entitled *Horatian Echo:*
and as it recalls more than one of Horace'

Odes, I asked Mr. Arnold, before sending a copy of the manuscript to the press, whether he would not like the title to be plural; or whether, if he preferred the singular, it should not be *An Horatian Echo.*

        Cobham, Surrey.   June 13th.
My dear Galton,
   Of course you may keep the Manuscript. I think I prefer the singular of Echo to the plural, in this case; but as you please. Will you tell the Editor that I received, and thank him for, his kind letter. I shall be interested in seeing your Cromwell. You have taken, I repeat, a really excellent subject.
      Ever yours truly, Matthew Arnold.

    Athenæum Club,
       Pall Mall, S.W.   June 15th.
My dear Galton,
   I have been looking at your letter again. If you make the title plural, you must not put Echos but Echoes. There speaks the-

ex–School–Inspector. But speaking as a composer, I really think the singular is preferable.

> *Ever yours truly, Matthew Arnold.*

> Cobham. 'June 18th.

My dear Galton,

I am going down into the north next week, and will take Cromwell with me. You have so good a subject that it would be a pity you should waste it;—and it would be wasting it, to employ it as a " bomb." However, from turning over the pages I hope that this expression of yours alarmed me unnecessarily. I will write and tell you what I think when I have read you. The dedication makes me a little apprehensive, for fear it should injure the book. Strong praise provokes many people; and this praise is strong, too strong. But if the book is good it will be able to stand even this dedication to a less than half popular author.

> *Ever truly yours, Matthew Arnold.*

114

Fox How,
    Ambleside.   June 23rd, 1887.
My dear Galton,
    *I have read your book through.   It has
many errors of the press, and your meaning
is not always made quite clear; but I have
been greatly interested, and the summing
up in the latter part of the volume I think
thoroughly good.   If I have done anything
to help you to the acquisition of the temper
and judgment there shown, I am glad.   I
still think your dedication may provoke
people, and be somewhat of an obstacle;
but men like Stubbs, and S. Gardiner, and
Freeman are the men whose judgment on
the book it is important to have, and I
cannot but believe they will be interested by
it.   I am only here for a day or two, and
shall then return to Cobham.*
            Ever yours truly, Matthew Arnold.

            Athenæum Club.   July 4th, 1887.
My dear Galton,
    *As I expected, Macmillan says he has of
course often thought of a single volume, but*

*thinks the time has not yet come. He is of
opinion that the sort of people who want my
poems are people who do not mind a high
price if they get a handsome book. The
case of Tennyson, he says, is " somewhat
different." I never have been broadly
popular, and I cannot easily bring myself
to believe I shall ever come so. But I
ought none the less to thank you for your
interest, and your kind letter.*

*The judgment of Stubbs is really prec-
ious; and that of Gladstone, if it could be
made public, would be the best of adver-
tisements. I was sure, after reading the
volume through, that you had done a good
piece of work. I hear to-day that Hans,
to whom I long to pay my respects, has
passed two good days, and seems settling
down in his new home.*

Ever truly yours, Matthew Arnold.

The following letter refers to a framed
copy of the picture, which Mr. Watts
gave to the January *Hobby Horse* for
1887.

Pains Hill Cottage,
     Cobham, Surrey.   July 11th.
My dear Galton,
     Very much thanks to you and to Mr.
Horne for the picture, which shows all
Watts' power. The numbers of the " Hobby
Horse" have arrived this morning. I
hope, but can hardly believe, that my little
bit of a thing may have been of some ser-
vice to you.
          Ever truly yours, Matthew Arnold.

Pains Hill Cottage,
     Cobham, Surrey.   Septr. 20th.
My dear Galton,
     I have found your letter and magazines,
on my return here.   I like both your art-
icles, though perhaps you are a little hard
on Macaulay—I have been a little hard
on him myself.   Such a wonderful corres-
pondence between the man and his medium,
as there was between Macaulay and the
age in which he lived and worked, has
hardly ever been seen; and what is provoking in him,—his cock sureness, his

117

boundless satisfaction,—could hardly have been otherwise under the circumstances. After all, he pays a penalty heavier than any which our disparagement can inflict upon him—the penalty that he can hardly be of use to any mortal soul who takes our times and its needs seriously.

What you say of Gladstone is very interesting. I am glad to hear what Gardiner says of your Cromwell; I hope you will make your monograph the nucleus for a large and solid piece of work.

Ever truly yours, Matthew Arnold.
. Hans is a perfect dear.

And so the letters end, with one of those intimate and delightful touches, which reveal and which endear the writer:

"Of little threads our life is spun,
And he spins ill, who misses one."

The admirable simplicity of Mr. Arnold's published writings, the urbanity and the kindliness of their manner, the buoyancy of their spirit, and the tenderness, " the

sense of tears," which is always to be
found in them, in spite of their buoyancy,
have brought him into a close and an intimate relation with innumerable readers;
even with readers, who did not know
him personally; for he had the art of
giving " so much which communicates
his own spirit and engages ours." So
winning and so abiding are these personal qualities in him, that many readers
have imagined an old and intimate friend
to be speaking to them ; and this intimacy has tempted some of them, it may
be, to over-look the power, the beauty,
and the perfection, which are never absent from his writings. Other readers,
it is evident, have been puzzled and
offended by the " Distinction " of Mr.
Arnold's work: by that undeniable
quality in him, of which " the world is
impatient; it chafes against it, rails at it,
insults it, hates it; it ends by receiving
its influence and by undergoing its law."
Others, again, have been seduced from
the perfect clearness and simplicity of

Mr. Arnold, by the miserable influences of this our Day; by the more luxuriant though coarser styles, or by the louder though emptier tones, or by the imposing obscurity, of its most fashionable performers in prose and verse. Though more and more, as times go on, the power, the beauty, and the perfection, of Mr. Arnold's work will be discerned; if it be true, that " nothing lives but style," then he should be, almost certainly in prose, and certainly in verse, the most living of our Victorian men of letters: and he should be no less permanent for his matter, than for his style; because the spirit of our time appears to have achieved in him, not only its most perfect, but its most complete, and its most representative expression; in his work, the finer intellectual movements of our Day are reflected in their greatest beauty and truth, and are represented with unequalled power. But although these high questions may be interesting to discuss, they are for the future only to decide; an author's contemporaries never have decided them, and never can decide them, finally : what Mr. Arnold's contemporaries can decide, is that they feel in his work those intimate and those endearing qualities, of which I have spoken. Those delightful qualities, if a writer have them, are to be found most perfectly in his letters; and this would be mine apology, were an apology required, for publishing these few letters : they show the kindness, the homeliness, and the unaffected simplicity of Mr. Arnold's bright and happy nature; and therefore I hope they may serve, in some small degree, to bring him nearer to those, who did not know him; that is, to make him more beloved and more fondly remembered. For those, who did know him, will not soon forget the charm of that gracious presence;

> " That comely face, that cluster'd brow,
> That cordial hand, that bearing free,
> I see them still, I see them now,
>   Shall always see ! "

121

never can they forget the fascination and
the happiness, which were communicated
by that buoyant though gentle spirit:
the fifteenth of April will come and go,
many times, before it ceases to dawn
upon a group of mourners, who are
inconsolable.

April: 1890.

[These Essays and Letters were first published
in the *Century Guild Hobby Horse*.]

www.ingramcontent.com/pod-product-compliance
Lightning Source LLC
Chambersburg PA
CBHW031157050726
47495CB00019B/2465